# A Slow Indwelling

Small Harbor Publishing

Cover art and design: Megan Merchant, "Evolution"
Interior design: Brianna Chapman
Editor: Beth Bolton
Publisher Allison Blevins
Executive Editor: Kristiane Weeks-Rogers
Managing Editor: R. B. Simon


A SLOW INDWELLING
MEGAN MERCHANT, LUKE JOHNSON
ISBN 978-1-957248-38-7
Harbor Editions,
an imprint of Small Harbor Publishing

# A Slow Indwelling

Poems by Megan Merchant
& Luke Johnson

Harbor Editions
Small Harbor Publishing

# A Slow Indwelling

# Contents

*open me carefully*

—Emily Dickinson

# What I want in these lines

is origin mist
& static.
Suspension

& stillness &
the body before
it shocks

with air—no air.
How the fingers
furl to fists

& the lips
creased
cage a howl,

the first
hacked
syllables of pain.

Did I tell you
mom collected
pulled molars

in coffee cans?
We'd find
them mixed

with pennies,
a few loose
strands of thread,

then shake
them like
recycled maracas

while swaying
to Bonnie Raitt.
Once,

after dad
embossed her
back—stink

like feral swine—
she whispered
my son

*collect the living*
*by grieving*
*lost things*

then split apart
in two.
Suppose I place

an unmet
promise
in a vacant house,

one clock
keeping
the elements.

Shadows
leap like jackals
& the light

like life
is small as seed—
a gale in an

unopened box.
You take it out
to dig a hole, M,

but the earth resists
& the box
continues to shake.

I refuse
to tell you what's inside
or why

it resists your offering.
When Cain
came near in his

brother's blood
the Lord let
out a scream

& on his skin
the lightening carved:
*here*

*is a curse*
*even I can't cleanse,*
*here*

*is an orphaned melody.*

*S*

# Crown Shyness

Have I told you yet how much I love the hawk-light,
the crown shyness of trees—the almost-touch if not

more than the *moment of* and the *moment after.* I love
scraping a black pen through damp paint, so it almost

reads, and the shade of blue that can't be pinned into
an hour. E.E. Cummings said *twice I have lived*

*forever in a smile* and Zelda Fitzgerald said *I remember*
*every single spot of light that ever gouged a shadow*

*beside your bones.* Some quotes are glyphs, others
blood cuts. We don't often empty the bottle, one-upping

each other with beautiful almosts. L, I would win.
Once there was an almost-empty room and steel

strings and that song, played in the sharpest corner,
it was as if gravity could predict such wreckage

and stayed half-asleep, the way I was until that moment.
Do you know why the branch tips don't touch? I do.

Here, the winter light is a collision of soft & ice. Here,
the rooms of the body are ravaged by fingerprints & feathers.

# But what about the carpenter ant,

who tunnels under trees to steal
the sap, leaves the roots exposed?

My daughter watches cormorants
scatter & says *blood* which sounds

like *flood*, waters receding slowly.
This, before the sick that floods her

stomach & spills, despite persistent
prayers, the pendants of holy saints.

I read a boy was taken by waters
while his mother foraged mushrooms

from rain-soaked forest. She said
the rain had stopped & birds returned,

that it *came from the hills so suddenly*.
M, Jung refused the need for levity.

Wrote *sentimentality is a super-structure
that covers brutality*. I too am guilty

of praising the hawk, of climbing
trees to convene with the weather.

But when my daughter asks me why
she bleeds, what do I tell her? What

good are my words when the Lord
won't answer them?

## Origin Story

My son stands at the morning kitchen,
asks *how were people created*?

He doesn't want the answer, wants the silence
that edges stumped questions. In our house,

god is more furnace than architect.
Yesterday, I bought a hatchet at the hardware

store, for slim branches spidering
low on our acre, and all I can imagine is it

slamming into my thigh. Metal, branch, bone.
Soon there will be nubs and shoots, the cold

hand of winter lifting. Soon we will have a pile
split and stacked for another freeze. My son asks

*how was the first tree made*? We trace its lineage
around the edges—body of my guitar, books, desk

where I write. Ghosts. From our window, grosbeaks
and buntings tangle into flight. The hours count

earlier now, because of the way they are lit.
When my children are grown, will they look

into the thicket of poems to find me? L, what
splinters have I left that will redden and ache?

# As the body breaks, it is whole,

or so the silent Buddhists write
when describing why children die

beneath burning rubble made
from war machines. I wish I was the father

who fought harder for peace,
who believed I too could trade

collective pain for promises.
Pilate withered when the chants

of three hundred crazies called
for Christ's head. The night before

his wife witnessed a warning
in a dream and came to him crying

*Let the rabbi go.* I go into grocery
stores followed by ghosts. My father, once,

in an empty aisle looking for frozen
cheesecake. My friend the next

with holes in his head, mopping
up spilled milk. M, why are the dead

so demanding? Why, when Christ
was nailed to die, did his mother

watch the thorns woven, her son
a slaughtered lamb? Listen: When I

said boys have a storm inside,
this itch that fills our teeth, I

was sharing in secret. I meant
we have mothers who gift us ghosts,

our heads upon a trigger.
We're bred to die. We're set

upon a foreign field
and asked to praise the blood.

# Mirror Test

There's a dead pigeon in a shoebox inside of my chest.
It lives there. I thought you should know. It's why

I keep weird closets of tenderness. A blonde horse tail
braided with ribbon. My ancestors' incisors in a jar.

Cracked opera glasses and a mug with lipstick claiming the rim.
I have tried to hold something of October, but the open

windows steal. I have tried to tell you things in these poems,
but maybe all I've done is construct well-worded armor.

That is why. The pigeon, L, was held in my mother's hands.
She nursed it with a syringe in her garage to secret it

from my father. She brushed its bent wings with her thumb,
It shit-splattered her favorite wool sweater. I could hear her,

at night, cooing next to the motor oil and broken lamp shades.
The perfume of spilled gas. The flowers on her dress so

slender they looked like axes or people leaning toward
each other with a secret. It was dark. The pigeon died.

And she did too. Some years the dark is full of teeth. Others,
it lets you go with a playful nip. What would happen

if I freed the bird from my chest? Outside, the trees are
rattling their leaves clean off.

# If I tell you when my mother speaks of love

the birds in the foreground
grow still,
would you believe me?

I remember his
cigar first
& after his smoke

a trail of fingernails
tangled in my hair.
How his stink

lingered months
on sheets & clothes
& how

she scrubbed tirelessly
into the evenings
to wipe his laughter away.

When I dream,
I yell his name,
& when I wake,

I hear him weeping.
He's ten & skinny
& hides

his head from
his father's gun.
Once on a walk,

as it started to rain
& sunlight slipped
from the leaves,

a single cardinal
flared the dark
& landed beside

a lingering blossom
tilted by the wind.
The oaks had long

let go their flowers
& curled themselves
toward earth.

I danced M,
like a lunatic son,
when a voice—

I swear to you—
started to speak,
said *let go loss*

*& wash clean.*
How foolish I am,
how desperate.

My clothes
left heaped
& body naked—

river brimming
with ice. As I
floated there weeping,

I remembered
the look
on her face while

he gasped.
How she smiled,
though I could

see her slipping,
how she lay
in his chest & let go.

# I explain absence to my husband,

there will be a day when I sit and write
with fever—I mean fervor, and again,

language betrays me, shanks the possibility
of reaching another. Every specialist we've

seen has said, *In order to understand the
ailment, you must first explain.* My son

refuses to leave the car while the other
mothers honk in line—his hysterics rooted

in feeling cold. *I have shivers,* he explains,
which, in the foreign wiring of his brain,

could mean hunger, or pain, or a tap of doubt
that he is enough for this day. The weather—

warm, his body armored in snow gear. I buckle
him back in and try to remember the lyrics

to a song he's been humming for weeks,
the one I've been blurring to keep room

in my head, for what, exactly, I don't know.
War. Fear. Fever. Maybe I loved the word

*melancholy* too much while I grew him, L,
maybe language is the one thing that allows

me to carry the blame. I sing the words
wrong, and wrong again. In his letters home

from war, my grandfather wrote about how,
under a ceiling of streaming ammunition,

the soldiers played broken instruments,
terribly. His fists unable to unfurl.

# Cold,

my daughter stands nude
in the moonlit kitchen
fevered by a dream

and starts to scream her
hands are burning boats,
mouth a mist of wasps.

She's been doing this lately.
Waking when her eyes are shut
and wandering out

to greet what whispers,
calling her by name.
The doctors say they start

in the mind, then move
through the body—
a virus eating its host.

It began sometime when
her mind was shaped,
suspended in the womb.

I want to sing a song
that shatters her shaking,
a psalm that sets her free.

But where is the Lord?
And why, when dreaming,
she cannot surface,

despite my desperate calls?

# When it doesn't rain,

I walk the night-city without shoes.
One night, someone left a wig on the bank

stairs and when I circled back, it had multiplied.
A nest. I imagined the people who tossed them

haphazard, no longer needing a disguise—
clumped strands that smelled like stale beer

and moonlight. A friend told me how a poem
is trying to be seen and hide at the same

time. One day, I woke and decided, after
all these years, I want to move home. Even

knowing the place has changed beyond me.
But my hands are bulbed and waiting to bloom—

they look like my mother's. I have one photo
where she is curling my hair, I was three,

and in awe of becoming. The world wasn't
yet an echo of dark around every corner.

The world wasn't what it is. I walk barefoot
hoping not to get cut too deeply. L, I do not

think of her when music drifts from bar
windows—a piano, even though she told

me about that summer she worked dancing
on one and singing. But when I cut my foot

on glass, and press the skin until blood
weeps—I look in that gash for her song.

# When it rains,

I take the torso
of a stringless guitar

to pretend pluck a song
for both my sons,

who squint in its sound hole
& imagine

it swirling—sucking
in fragments of stars.

*Black hole*, one of them says
& the other: *gun barrel*,

& for a moment my hands
go hot with fear,

fighting back fevers of war.

Yesterday,
a drone ripped through

an orphanage in Northern Ukraine
& a dog emerged

with a mouthful of ash, begged
the camera for a drink.

The host stretched his hand
to soothe the dog

& the dog, though desperate,
shrunk back snarling,

threatened those who neared.

I once watched
my boys rummage

river stones to uncover
their blurred reflections

& discover, while digging,
an abandoned gun,

scuffed by wood drift & silt.
That night

they buried the gun in a box
& set their ears

against the grass
to listen to its snarl.

All night I gnashed
my teeth, wrestled God,

and when he threw
my hip like he did Jacob,

curled beneath
his burning haze,

who dared another dance.
In days

my sons would hold
their books

and hope
that when

a bullet
spun,

it wedged inside
the words.

# What do we do when the black hole comes,

my son asks before the hours lighten. L, I know so much of this life
is unreal, but yesterday I cut my lip and flooded my mouth

with blood. I read about parents who chew food then mama-bird
it into their babies' mouths so they won't choke. Haven't I been

doing this with the world? I have cellophaned windows and boarded
the doors to keep them safe, clammed the news

with Vivaldi, given his finger-guns shadows until they grew into
beaks on the blank wall. And still,

a war rages, our entanglement of invisible threads. News makes
it across about a mother who shielded her infant with her back

while the shells burst and another who braved her way into the front-
line rubble of her house to play a piano one last time—the notes

ricocheting across glass and splintered wood. If I say I am most
afraid of people, don't I also mean ourselves? Instead, I say

*unimaginable*, because there is distance. I tell my son the nearest
black hole is 3,000 light years away, while here, it is spring outside.

The trees blast pollen—the yellow shrapnel coats everything. I sneeze
so loud the birds shit-scatter. Without a second thought, we pile

heavy books to kill spiders that lumber between sheets, not even looking
to see if their abdomens are swollen with eggs.

# When my daughter, not yet three

turns to study the contours of my face & says
*I see you* says: *how long before the stars burn out*

which startles me, morphs her hands to hardness,
a variable chill, I say never say: *sometimes all we*

*have is this* & turn her toward my chest to spare
confusion. I fear, of course, the world dear M,

& cannot stomach sorrow—all the ways a child
drowns like spiders trapped in spit. I read a story

of a simple priest who stopped to sleep in a garden
at noon & woke beside a wolf in snow who curled

to keep him warm. The day before, the priest
paused to praise an opening dahlia & placed

its blue flame in his hair while undressing
by a stream. Sequined light, shadows of spring

clouds smeared by wind, he washed beneath
the Spanish moss & watched the flower fall

away—his secret lost to sin. When the dream
was over, the wolf was gone, & the priest began

to weep. When my daughter touched my fearful
face, I too began to weep. I read the story alone

in a room of a church made blue by rain. My
mother moved among its worn pews wiping

away the dust. We were poor & without grace.
I was without grace & groaning with blue. On the walls,

the children hung papered stars, wrote prayers
in sparkled paint. One of them asked the Lord

for a pony, another for a million bucks to rebuild
Noah's ark. But one of the stars was without name,

its prayer crossed out with blue. My brother hiding—
the boy without a spoken name who plays a quiet cello.

# It has been so hard to write,

let alone breathe. I go to work concerned
    my son will find a phone in a field while

he runs from gunfire and forget my number.
    M, today my wife attended my daughter's

awards ceremony and sent a video of her
    too afraid to stand. The look on her face:

confused. She wakes in sweats at night,
    screams when bullets spill from her mouth

like spiders and dissipate into the floor.
    As a boy, I'd watch my mother toss seeds

to city streets. I'd wait until she'd arrive home,
    weeping for a brother I never knew, a boy

not born, his name a serrated knife, then
    hand her water and a little blue pill to put

her soundly to sleep. By spring the streets
    would flare with copper, bees arrived,

and my mom walked with her hand
    outstretched as though holding someone else's.

And now I hold onto what is slipping. I ask
    my son to show me how he hides and critique

if I hear breathing, demand my daughter
    press her head to my heart and hold until

the static stops. The swell of our blood in sync—

# Blanket Flowers

Before my aunt died from breast cancer,
she held dinner for her closest,

gave me wrapping paper laced with seeds
I couldn't bring myself to sprout.

What gift is worthy enough to swaddle?
When my children were little, I wore them

in wraps, their tiny fists and elbows bruised
my breastbone and ribs, the straps secured

enough they wouldn't slip. I counted their
breaths even, refused to let the world have

them, yet. Today, we watch lizards and marvel
at how their tails regrow if caught under tread

or cinched between teeth. Powers we want,
in case. The closest I've come is the skin

around my c-section scar that regrew—a power
line, buried. The dig site, closed. I've read that

some schools, after shootings, remain open.
Others ghost into a vacant grief. L, I wish I could

tell you there's a way to move forward, but I've
forgotten how to construct a prayer as if it actually

helps. I take photos of dead flowers instead. Their
red—rusted deep, the jar of water tinged like piss.

A flower my son picked for me on the last day
of school. When he let it drop into my palm,

he asked how long it might survive.

# Poem After Listening to Chris Cornell & Learning of my Mother's Heart Attack

Mushrooms wrap a felled oak,
find food in cracks where rain

has festered. Where my mom, M,
would walk alone and wait to see

my brother, the boy she aborted,
rise from weeds          and flicker

like tempered glass. On days
when he would kiss her lips

to blow his rot inside her, she'd
arrive home with her pockets

full and do as my ancestors said:

1.  Set a suitcase by the door
    with shoes and socks,
    a coat for colder nights.

2.  Do not wash, not ever.
    It rips the pulp so flesh is dulled
    and leads to leaky centers.

3.  De-stem but do so gently.

4.  Knead the bulbs like babies scalps
    and squeeze until the heat and
    sweat erupt aroma—
    sigh it through your nose.

5.  Boil.

6.  Slip into a scalding bath
    and rub them on a wound.

7.  Weep.

8. After the bath, ingest one whole and ask it to detach the dead.

9. Air dry in the open dark.

10. Ignore your living son.

11. Stand by the window to scan for life.

12. Ignore your living son.

# Ghost Words

: a word that is not actually used but is recorded in a dictionary or other
reference work.

I have dreams that my unborn
are arranged on eight
silver platters,

a bouquet of mushrooms
and mint harvested
from our yard

the year
our house fell.

The table long, a single
wooden chair.

All of them, unnamed.
I am asked to sit and feast.

The only way to bring them
back to me.

I haven't told you this before—
but, after they sliced the tumor
from her brain,

my mother's final words
on this earth were
*you are just too difficult to be loved*,

punctuated by the meds bleeping
into her veins, tubes snaking
clairvoyant.

A psychic told me she wasn't in her
right mind and to forget.

But it's as if, in that cold hospital
room, I swallowed a single
dark strand of her hair
and now it strangles.


L, I'm tired of loving what leaves me
unloved.


In my dream, the chef comes and asks
if everything is arranged
thoughtfully enough
to make it beautiful.

The blood clots, the soft tissue.
The stilled heartbeats.

I have been refusing to see.


It's true—some pain
raws behind grief,
waits patiently in the body.


If you want to know how
I found it, follow the raised
outline made by the tip of a knife.

It's the place where my screams
unsound.

# Like Ruin

We could talk about the baby humpback who washed ashore with a belly of trash and a net used for catching thousands of fish. How children circled to see its slick skin flake in the sun of California and the birds, so many of them, glob flesh then raise it back like ruin, one after the other after the other. We could stand around watching the wonder dim as sea diminishes, while parents snap photos and point and crawl into its gaping mouth to pull out giant teeth. But yesterday, while my daughter danced in a dead field, flowers choked by soot, my son came running with a bullet in his hand and before I had time to take it, stuck it in his mouth and said it tasted like lemons. Kant would argue a seed of violence spreads in silence until, too late, a boy is beckoned to break apart beauty and scatter it. That as it blooms, his song diminishes and all chances for goodness are gone. That night I put the bullet in a pocket of mud, and as I planted it, heard my son cry, the sting on his tongue: throbbing. Why am I telling you this? I stood before the shell of that beast on that day in July and whispered *sorry* as I told my son *spit*, his mouth flooded with ruin. Imagined its mother a mile off the coast, circling—her panicked calls. Nothing but shadows and shadows.

# Obituary

I thought of you and bullets and the husk of ruin we are feeding
our children, saying *swallow, it will make you strong in the end,*

but I know. When I sat the other day with my own loneliness—
as I have been taught—near people, but not, I listened to them

ask about one of their group, who was missing. *Dead. Fell off
a ladder.* They laughed, & it was true. One man said *I hope*

*he suffered before he passed. He should have known better.*
Then they swapped stories of near-misses and dumb decisions

they should not have survived. Plugging a router into an amp.
Stringing holiday lights in the rain. I guess it's hard to know

which side of balance we are on. Until it's not. I'd like to stay
on the opposite shore of cruelty for as long as I can, which is

why I was sitting alone, why I'm teaching my son to swim,
to keep his head bobbled above enough to breathe.

The night my mother passed, I dreamt the town was flooded
and she was alone in a room, wallpaper peeling as if the print

of yellow daisies were windswept, not wilting. She was waiting
in a wooden chair, a concerto echoing through the walls. When

I asked how long, she said days. Water up to her knees.
I was the one who carried her home. When I got home,

I looked up the man's obituary and, L, I kid you not, he was on
that ladder trying to save a cat from a too-high branch before

the storm folded into flood. Do you think he tasted lightning
before it struck? What if the last thing we taste of this world

are lemons? Not bitter, not rust, but one placed in a white bowl
on the counter. The light around it loudening yellow.

The rush of juice dissolving to the last sprinkle of sugar.

40

A kindness. A single note held on a violin.

## Olivia Rodrigo, Van Gogh, This Viscous Light

Today, while my daughter sang of damaged hearts
    & son laid curled in the backseat, a sunbird swerved
        through spindled light & splattered on the hood.
           My son began to scream. And as he screamed,
        my daughter hummed, nodding to the beat.
    Van Gogh believed to hear one breathe
was far more precious than sight. So he carved his ear
    in a birthday box & autographed the back. Reports
        vary of course, & the gift fades to legend. Lovers
           claim she strung the ear to an almond tree
    & watched it sway with snow, others
    that it was wrapped in twine & buried by his grave.
When my lover writhed, I hid my gaze, afraid to watch
    her crown. Her lips blue & body limp, cord a pulsing
        noose. Until a single slap released a howl that calmed
           when latched to suckle. I swear, M,
           the problem is rage.
        We fear, too often, *I love you*. The buzz
    in our ears a buzzsaw of fates, swarming for release.
My son saw the impact, its breaking shoulder,
    & begged to leave the dream. I longed to leave it too.
        In days, my daughter would bleed & cripple, crawl
           into the quiet. Not even the trees would stir.
                Not even the birds.

## Internal Medicine

The same day I say there are no new poems in me,
my body attacks itself, refuses food in crampy tantrums—

except for apples. I have always said I feel most alive in the fall,
but this new craving makes no sense, makes all of the equations

of illness unsolvable. Despite the idiom, very little can be cured
by Gala, Honeycrisp, Red Delicious. It's what my body wants,

without consent. I see a series of doctors with the same schoolgirl
shame I've metabolized for years—men who want to palpate the pain

with their own hands, stick cameras in every angle to photograph
my interior. When sedated, I drug-dream the most beautiful paintings—

bruised ochre, opiate blue. A woman being carved thin by an invisible
hand. *You look good*, the nurse tells me, when I come to, *you've lost

weight*. When asked what concerns I carry, I tell her—not covid or cancer,
but the way I'm accepting what it's like to live with a punishing hunger.

*A slow indwelling*, as you say, L. Sculpting want into dead air.

# Tinderbox

I dig a hole to hide his box
& plant blue geranium.
I wait for rain, even in summer,
& will not turn my face
from the window.
To turn it means the Lord
is lost. The stars? Silent wicks.

Let me begin again.

In summer, when snow melts
slow from the San Gabriels
& pollen foreplays the fields,
I dip my thumb in paint
to press each star on parchment.
I scribble my name with charcoal.
Turn bone-char into sticky flowers
& imagine breath the billowing gale
that feeds his cold economy.

A medium once told me,
to return the dead,
one must crouch above
a body of water & swirl
until what stares back smiles.
But what about parchment
over candles & the way
each star is winnowed like wings, lost
from falling moths?

I dig a hole, M,
& fill it in with wind fall.
Subdue his scratch
to dirt—promise nothing.
At dusk, I hear a whistle
& wander out to find it.
For a moment, there is fear,
the sweetness of loss,
& shadows that somersault air.
Then the rain. Then the absence of it.

## Somatic Memory

I trap moths in a cardboard box, complain
that what lures them makes my sweaters

stink like a cigar stub left to the rain.
Why do you want to return the dead?

I leave the light on in a room one away.
Still, my ghosts tip over a window box

of blue-veined flowers, show their long
fingers as brittle light in winter. Some

days, I cough my mother's ashes from
my throat. L, it's possible to spend this life

trying to solve the arithmetic of longing,
find the one word that does not risk

pulling me under. Maybe that word is *god*.

When the surgeon excised my gallbladder,
I prayed—worried he'd clip a nerve fished

from the language center in my brain
or staple the artery that feeds the way

I see the world. Some people believe
memories are stored in fascia. Others think

we stockpile them in marrow and grief,
if we bend our bodies long enough—

they will release. If this is true, how will
I know the fine details of what I've lost?

I slump in the middle, write my son's spelling
words on the mirror in red. He memorizes

the way they make him feel, the order in which
they tell their own stories after he turns out the light.

# "How Bullets from an AR-15 Blow the Body Apart"

My son takes my hand in the checkout line, "You know, because of the world," he explains. *Here, the blast destroys large veins that carry blood back to the heart.* "This is what memories are made of," my grandfather told me the day we walked the shoreline, picked up broken shells to fill mason jars that lined his basement window. *A single bullet lands with a shock wave intense enough to blow apart a skull.* We buy candles that smell like ocean encased in glass, wonder about their burn-time. *Causes torrential bleeding that is quickly lethal.* My son cannot decide between helping me carry them to the car and keeping ahold of my hand. *Your body will literally tear apart.* When a raven shadows overhead, we pause to watch its wingspan knock out the sun. *A speed that would cross six football fields in a second.* They mimic shrill alarms. *Bone shatter. The impact is even more acute on the compact body of a small child.* I drive the slow way home, meander past playgrounds that glint with empty slides. *As the bullet slows down, that energy is so massive it has to go someplace.* L, that night, I dreamt that I was opening an email from his school: In the event of an emergency, the school will text you the address of the reunification center. Where, if you are lucky, you will have the chance to put your child's body back together.

*Italicized lines are from "The Blast Effect: This is how bullets from an AR-15 blow the body apart" that appeared in *The Washington Post*.

# Tether

I was 16
when I pressed
the trigger

of an air soft
and felt it
thrust forward

and felt it
winnow when
the blue jay

plummeted
forty feet
from pine

and started
flipping
like sparks

from a live M-80.
A burst that blew
the thumb

from the neighbor's
nephew
and later

left him unable
to write
or hold his lover's

hand.
It's true before
I wept,

I held
the bird
and examined

where
the pellet
entered,

but I refuse
to own the lie
that boys

find pleasure
in breaking things.
Believe me:

For days I
kept the bird
in a sealed

oak box
and before I
could bury it,

begged it to wake,
to re-seed song
in its throat.

Thrilled,
my son leads me
through the zoo

and points
to where piranha eat,
the heads

of feeders floating.
Fact: every year
in Argentina

three boys
fall in infested waters,
are stripped

while trying
to swim.
Fact: 90%

of amputees
still feel their
severed limb.

Sometimes we lose
what's most
important to us

and fill it in
with phantoms.
Scientists call

it muscle memory,
the mind re-mapping
neurons.

But what do we
make of those
we've lost

standing in the rain?
When my father
died, I smelled his cigars,

could hear him
clear his throat.
If I play his

favorite hit
he speaks in parable,
proposes

hide and seek.
I'm avoiding
where I planted

the bird, M,
I'm too afraid
to tell you.

So instead,
let's watch
the feeders swarm

and awe at how
my son smiles
while pointing to a fin.

## A writer says, *do not confuse the important with the urgent:*
### *From Min Jin Lee's keynote address at AWP 2023*

I look in the mirror. What it shows back—
urgency stitched together—bone wire, mother-watch,
paint smudge, oven heat, alarm of snow shadowing us tight,
split wood, ink belly, tuft of fur that lifts in a room with
closed windows. L, the dog died in my arms. I light
candles, bite down on songs. Once I saw a man's body
being pulled from a ravine, they tethered him to a bridge
of rush hour traffic. The cars made a bottleneck symphony.
Headlights glancing into clots of dark. A fill-in-the-blank.
We are all in passing. I covered the dog with my grandmother's
patchwork quilt. Her paws, in prayer, begged into my mind.
Now, I sew the button-eye back onto my son's rag doll to ready
it for night-watch, safe keeping. L, the dog slept on my feet,
a sustain pedal, ringing out light.

# St. Veronica

*She suffered a great deal under the care of many doctors, yet instead of getting better she grew worse.* —Mark 5:26

Once, after hide & seek in the neighboring estuary, where my son pretended himself a shadow & did not speak nor move for forty minutes, a time that caused me tremendous torment, I drew a bath at dusk to calm, & felt a hand shove my face toward water then hold until I could no longer breathe. I had been thinking of dead kids in school & death by drowning & how a body bloats before the buzzards clean up. My daughter by now was cursed with bleeds & her skin pure as porcelain, though more like colorless clay. When the pain was bad it came in shrieks & once after the final shriek, when she no longer spoke nor responded to her name, blew a window out above me. In truth it was a rock & my son, afraid of a beating, crept between two thin pines & contorted his body to look like bark. I've never laid a hand upon him. Not once. Not in that way. Though I have laid a hand in prayer & asked my ancestors to instruct him in the way of tenderness, in what Madame Guyon calls obscure illumination, one woven by force & ease like wind & blizzard. Like rain, when in a flash a flood snaps pines, converts to powdered ponds. When the hand let go, I gagged for voice & there my daughter stood. She was quiet & shivering & asking for a drink. I never considered if she was who tried to drown me. Not once. I've always thought I slipped between the surface as I started to dream & before I faded, she pulled me out,

the air our constellation.

# A Wake of Vultures

A housefly lives for twenty-eight days,
        one swirls our kitchen,
my son tries to chopstick its paper wings
        while it rains, L,
I have given you so many moments
        in these poems,
I search for more as a wake of vultures
        circle overhead—
road-scrum, picked-bones, nest fibers untwined
        in wind, *where have I been*
*hiding,* my son asks in the held-breath quiet
        closet / pantry / large box
that shimmies slightly when he laughs,
        we make a game of finding
each other *again, again.*

In the broad wing of the night, a guttural cry
        splices my sleep—lightning
storm, seizure. There are other words I've
        given it—*Quake. Déjà vu.*
                                        *Thief.*

*Where have I been hiding?* It will take days
        for his nervous system
to calm, to recall hunger and the nickname
        he'd given the dog,
to remember it died weeks ago. Then, grief—
        *again, again.*

Maybe if we spread the ashes into the creek
        bed, let them wind
around stones and sediment, make a song
        downstream.
                        Maybe

if we can find a splint of sun—then the turkey
        vultures can pause
their dark-watch long enough to widen
        their wings to dry, and

I will find him after counting *one, two*
       *three*—
the round white rescue pill put back
       into the bottle,
the windows opened like a sigh, like relief.

# Just like that

my daughter
     says she dreams
          of hands
and clocks
          and no matter
            her *no,*
how they grapple her legs
     and tug
          until she's drowning

under a surface
        of boys
             who are boys
              who are men

who are boys
        who scream
          to sublet
                  their rage.

*S*

# Keeping Time

*We grieve the living by collecting lost things.* I enter a vacant
house through the smallest window. Wedge poems under
the floorboards—where there was flood, or a dropped vase,

dents made from dancing. A waltz to slow time. When we
moved from ours, my son screamed until we shifted the last
bookcase from the wall so he could rescue a toy he knew

had slipped months before. A plastic spider he'd won at a carnival.
What he could not leave behind. Is what we prescribe to hold meaning
really a litany of fear? Why I clutch sorrow, search out words to give

to you—my mother's hair loosened in a storm, the horses' faces
veiled with masks. The snake that uncoiled from the flowerbed
to sun by the barn door, I ran it clean through under tires,

watched it slither away, halved. A correspondence of pain.
But also—it lived. L, these poems are entombed with lilacs
and bullet casings. Churched with wings.

# Acknowledgements

Thank you to the following journals where these poems first appeared:

*Pedestal*

*Stonecoast Review*

*The Hunger*

*West Trade Review*

*Indianapolis Review*

*One: A Journal of Jacar Press*

*Vox Populi*

*Heavy Feather Review*

*Shō Poetry Journal*

*Sky Island*

Megan Merchant (she/her) is the owner of www.shiversong.com and holds an M.F.A. degree in International Creative Writing from UNLV. She is the author of three full-length collections with Glass Lyre Press, four chapbooks, and a children's book, *These Words I Shaped for You* (Penguin Random House). Her book, *Before the Fevered Snow*, was released in April 2020 with Stillhouse Press (NYT New & Noteworthy). She was awarded the 2016-2017 COG Literary Award, the 2018 Beullah Rose Poetry Prize, the Inaugural Michelle Boisseau Prize and most recently the New American Poetry Prize. She is the Editor of *Pirene's Fountain*. You can find her poems and artwork at meganmerchant.wixsite.com/poet.

Luke Johnson is the author of *Quiver* (Texas Review Press), a finalist for the Jake Adam York Award, The Vassar Miller Prize, and The Levis Award; *A Slow Indwelling* (Harbor Editions 2024); and *Distributary* (Texas Review Press 2025). *Quiver* was recently named one of four finalists for The California Book Award. Johnson was selected by Patricia Smith as a finalist for the esteemed 2024 Robert Frost Residency through Dartmouth College. You can find more of his work at *Kenyon Review*, *Prairie Schooner*, *Narrative Magazine*, *Poetry Northwest* and elsewhere.

*S*

# Advance Praise

In this superb series of epistolary poems, Luke Johnson and Megan Merchant probe the fears and anxieties they face as loving parents in a fraught world. Their exchanges are marked by a lyricism that constantly surprises—L wants a dead bird to "re-seed song / in its throat"; M writes that "some years the dark is full of teeth." In lines that seem emblematic of the whole, L writes, for his daughter besieged by illness, "I want to sing a song / that shatters her shaking, a psalm that sets her free." There is sorrow in these exchanges, but there is also beauty, an uncompromising need for truth.

—Lynne Knight, author of *The Language of Forgetting*

In this remarkable collaborative book of meditations on family, illness, parenthood, and the fragility of living things, Johnson and Merchant have penned a polyvocal tome in language that pushes against the pain and replaces it with tender musical testaments: a beautiful duet that waltzes back and forth, page after page, "Churched with wings."

—Sean Thomas Dougherty, author of *Death Prefers the Minor Keys*

Luke Johnson and Megan Merchant have created a new treasure for readers of poetry. How wonderful it is to encounter a truly unique book—a weaving of two voices, two psyches, two ways of looking at the world, out of which has come this gorgeous wreath of poems. Open this book—with care, with tenderness—and find the many voices inside you speaking with one another, asking great questions, searching for truth in an endlessly lush dialectic, and loving the search.

—Joseph Fasano, author of *The Last Song of The World*

# About Small Harbor Publishing

Small Harbor Publishing is a 501c3 nonprofit organization. Our goal is to publish unique and diverse voices. We are a feminist press, and we are committed to diversity and inclusion. We strive to bring new voices to a devoted and expanding readership.

Small Harbor Publishing began in 2018 with the first issue of *Harbor Review*. The magazine is an online space where poetry and art converse. *Harbor Review* quickly grew and now publishes reviews and runs multiple micro chapbook competitions, including the Washburn Prize and the Editor's Prize.

In July 2020, Small Harbor Publishing was officially incorporated and began Harbor Editions. Harbor Editions accepts submissions through a chapbook open reading period, a hybrid chapbook open reading period, the Marginalia Series, and the Laureate Prize.

In 2023, Harbor Anthologies began with a mission to promote texts that explore social justice issues and highlight marginalized writers.

If you would like to support Small Harbor Publishing, please visit our "About" page at smallharborpublishing.com/about.

www.ingramcontent.com/pod-product-compliance
Lightning Source LLC
Chambersburg PA
CBHW020216090426
42734CB00008B/1097